Cumbria Way

Jason Friend

Zymurgy
Publishing

This book is dedicated to Lynette Whitehouse, whose support, advice and encouragement has made this project possible.

First published in Great Britain by
Zymurgy Publishing in 2006.

Design and layout by Nick Ridley

A CIP catalogue record for this book is available from the British Library.

Printed by Compass Press Limited

10 9 8 7 6 5 4 3 2 1

ISBN 1-903506-20-4

Zymurgy Publishing
Newcastle upon Tyne

Contents

Foreword

The county of Cumbria in the north-west corner of England has attracted many generations of visitors. Tourism is thriving and arguably is now Cumbria's most important industry. The designation of the Lake District National Park in 1951 helped to fuel the popularity of the area. Many people come to enjoy the peace and tranquility to be found on mountains, in valleys, at lakeside and along the coast. The challenge and exhilaration of hiking through Cumbria's magnificent countryside is why many people come to Cumbria.

The landscape that we now walk, was at one time subject to violent volcanic eruptions, glaciations and submergence under the sea. Over the last few hundred years agriculture has had the most significant effect on landscape development. Without agriculture there would not be villages and market towns, moorland for grazing, dry stone walls and stone buildings. Today, the natural processes of wind, rain, snow and ice, plus thousands of hiking boots are having an impact. In the future, changes to agricultural subsidies may lead to sheep leaving the high fells and result in significant changes to the terrain.

In the 1970s The Ramblers Association realised that many walkers and visitors were concentrating on 'hot spots' within the county, places like Windermere, Scarfell and Hellvelyn. They decided to construct a route using existing paths to introduce people to some of the less well known parts of the county, The trail is Cumbria's longest path, it starts in the south of the county near the sands of Morecombe bay, heads slowly north through arguably some of the finest scenery to be found in the Lake District National Park before completing its course in at the county town - the City of Carlisle. The Cumbria Way can be walked in sections, a day at a time over several months, or all in one go in under a week.

About the Cumbria Way

The Cumbria Way meanders some seventy miles from the market town of Ulverston in the south of the Lake District Peninsulas to the historic Cumbrian capital of Carlisle in the north. The 'Way' must be considered as one of the finest walks in the British Isles, although it is not officially designated as a long distance route. The reason official recognition has not been established is the complexity and length of time involved (in the case of the Pennine Way it took several decades).

The Ramblers' Association planned a route which would allow the walker to fully enjoy the spectacular and picturesque landscape to be encountered in the county. By devising a route that used existing rights of way and small country lanes, they were able to avoid legal red tape and quickly introduce the walk that is now well established. The route predominately follows many tranquil Lakeland valleys, with only a couple of high and exposed mountain passes.

Often problems are encountered on unofficial routes since waymarking can be sketchy in some places, but anyone with map reading skills is unlikely to experience any serious problems navigating the Cumbria Way.

That is not to say that the Cumbria Way is necessarily a simple walk. The first hurdle is its very distance. Seventy miles is a sizeable achievement for any walker and the correct equipment is essential. As it is a multi-day ramble, walkers must carry spare clothing, food and equipment. Those intending to camp en route need to take a decent but lightweight tent, sleeping bag and associated gear. The fickle weather often encountered in the Cumbrian fells will also provide a challenge.

It may be possible to walk the complete length without any rain or wind, although from my experience I would say that this is highly unlikely. Prepare yourself for the worst!

There are many choices of accommodation along the Way. In my opinion, camping is by far the most pleasurable way to fully immerse oneself in the Cumbrian landscape, although the walker seeking creature comforts will not be disappointed by the typically high standards of friendly Cumbrian hotels, guest houses and bed & breakfasts. The Way was designed to be a five-day route with four overnight stays, but personally I would recommend breaking the sections down further to ensure that you have time to fully appreciate the splendour of Cumbria's hills and the Lake District National Park.

One final decision that must be made before setting out on the Cumbria Way is to choose which direction you should walk. The 'official' recommendation from the Ramblers' Association is to walk the route from south to north, so that the prevailing winds will hopefully be from behind as you head towards Carlisle.

Having walked the Way on numerous occasions in both directions, I have decided to cover it in the direction suggested by the Ramblers' Association, although I do feel that there are many benefits for walking it in the reverse direction. It cannot be denied that the Carlisle stretch of the route does not really make a fitting end to the Way, although admittedly the Ramblers' Association is continuing to develop this stretch and to enhance the last few miles by re-routing it. Following it southwards allows you to have prolonged views of spectacular landscapes that may be missed when following it in the traditional direction. Ulverston also makes a far more agreeable finale.

Perhaps the ideal solution is to plan two trips, walk it in both directions, and then draw your own conclusions! However, whichever direction you choose to walk the Way you will be rewarded with an unforgettable journey through what many consider to be England's finest landscape.

A break in storm clouds illuminates the Mickleden and surrounding Langdale mountains.

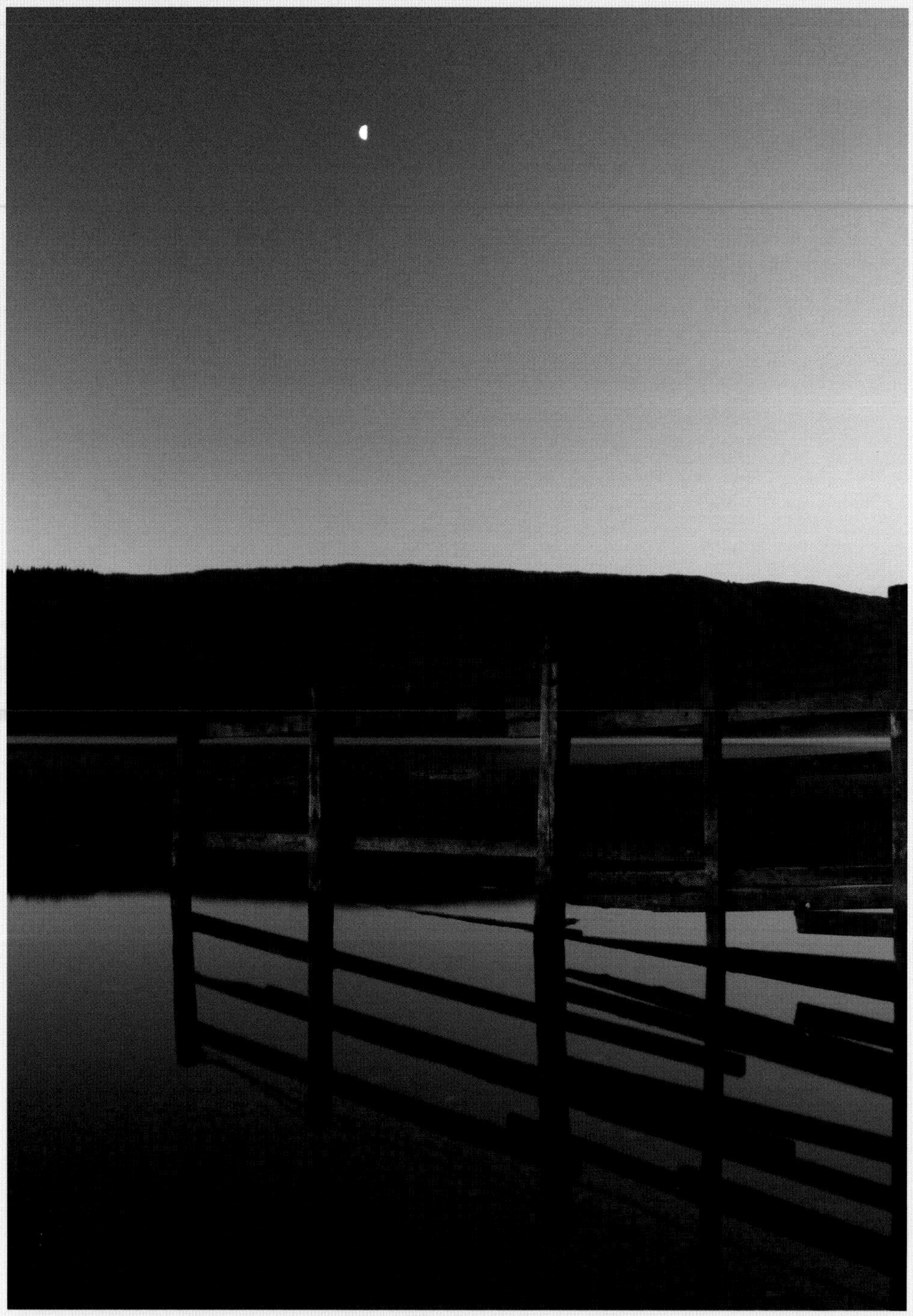

A wooden fence along the shores of Coniston Water, reflected in the still expanse of the lake.

A winter study of tussock and ice on the banks of Whit Beck.

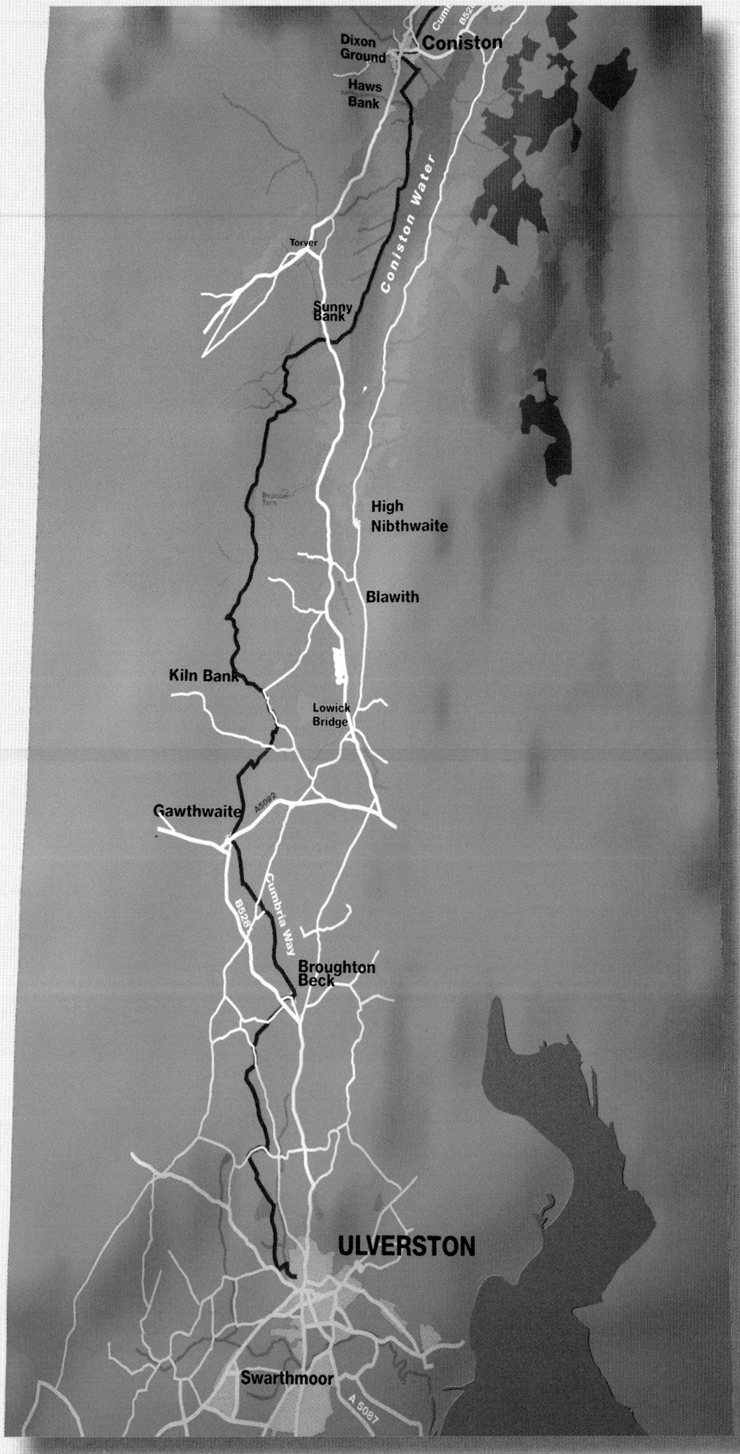
Dixon Ground
Coniston
Haws Bank
Coniston Water
Torver
Sunny Bank
High Nibthwaite
Blawith
Kiln Bank
Lowick Bridge
Gawthwaite
A5092
B5281
Cumbria Way
Broughton Beck
ULVERSTON
Swarthmoor
A 5087

Ulverston to Coniston

Ulverston is a small, friendly market town situated close to Morecambe Bay, in what has become known as the Lake District Peninsulas. It is famous for its local street market, which is entwined with the history of the town. The Thursday market has been held every single week since 1280, with the exception of one day when the town was in the grip of the plague. Somewhat more recently, a street market has been introduced on a Saturday, bringing a further sense of community to this small but lively town.

The cotton industry played a major part in shaping the history of Ulverston. The mile-long canal linking the south east of the town to the Leven Estuary was constructed in 1796, during a period when the original port was engulfed by silt. The canal was engineered by John Rennie and was considered to be the shortest, deepest and widest cut canal in Britain. It was built to meet the demand for exports from the region, which were mainly slate, gunpowder, malt and sailcloth. This exchange of trade meant that raw cotton arrived in Ulverston, destined for the area's new spinning mills. The canal was eventually sealed off from the Irish Sea in 1949, creating an ideal wildlife environment.

Ulverston is the birthplace of Stan Jefferson, or Stan Laurel as he was to become, which has put it on the map. There is a plaque on the house where the comic genius was born which proudly states 'Stan Laurel was born in this house in 1890'. Between 1926 and 1952 Ulverston's favourite son starred in more than one hundred ' Laurel and Hardy' films and entertained audiences all over the world.

Perhaps for some it is the location of the town that is its main appeal. The picturesque Morecambe Bay laps its southern boundaries, whilst the distant Cumberland hills and mountains can be seen to the north. It is also the start of the Cumbria Way, the head of the route being identified by a sculptured needle, complete with examples of the various kinds of rock to be found along the trail. The small plaque beside the beck ahead is the true start of the track, and contains the simple inscription 'Gillbanks, Start of the Cumbria Way'.

The Cumbria Way track starts as a gentle stroll alongside a small beck running through a pocket of deciduous woodland. The town's industrial development was heavily dependent upon this watercourse to provide water power for the mills. Now a firm bitumen track runs beside the beck for approximately a quarter of a mile before a signpost heralds the route's turn to the left. Here all thoughts of the track being a gentle stroll for seventy-odd miles are dispelled as it climbs abruptly and an uneven path begins underfoot. It is here that the characteristic aroma of the Lake District becomes apparent, a smell so quintessentially English that it is virtually impossible to describe. Following the walled path that nestles between woodland and fields, walkers are gradually introduced to a natural environment which is in stark contrast to the town left behind. After passing through a narrow gap in the dry stone wall to the right, the route continues through fields towards a farmhouse and its first meeting with the agricultural world of the Cumbrian hills.

Passing the farmhouse, a small gate and a sign continue the Way to the left, preceding a steep ascent through farmed fields alongside more broad-leaved woodland. Looking back towards the town, this slightly strenuous climb provides rewarding views over the shimmering Irish Sea in early sunlight and the sheer expanse of Morecambe Bay. The views become even better as the path branches right past a wonderfully located house, over a stile in the wall and across the open field to another stile. Here, the views really open up as the distinct features of the Yorkshire Dales and Pennine Hills can be identified in the distance on a clear day. In the summer months it is not only the views that are impressive, as this small patch of uncultivated land becomes a blanket of colour with a glorious display of wild flowers.

From here the Way continues across farmland used for grazing cattle until it reaches Higher Lath Farm, from where it then alternates between minor public roads and rights of way across farmland. After passing through Hollowmire (particular attention is needed in the summer months in order not to miss a right turn concealed by overgrown vegetation), the route heads towards the landmark of a distant church and continues along the left side of the cemetery wall.

After passing beside the small picturesque church of St John, the route follows a minor country lane fringed by well-established native hedgerows that provide a habitat for a variety of wildlife. During the spring and summer months, it is possible to observe bees on their never-ending quest for pollen, and butterflies searching for nectar. The route soon passes through the small village of Broughton Beck, before once again entering land used for grazing cattle. This stretch of the Way is largely flat and easily navigable, meandering through typical English countryside before it reaches a small country lane. After a left and immediate right turn along a public driveway, complemented by a reassuring 'Cumbria Way' sign, the route climbs slightly until it finally reaches the small settlement of Gawthwaite.

Following the rustic signs, walkers will discover a change on entering the Lake District National Park. Created in 1951 and covering an area equivalent to 880 square miles, this was once the largest national park in the whole of Britain, but after the recent formation of the Cairngorms National Park in Scotland, it can now only claim to be the largest in England. There is a common misconception that land within the park is owned by the National Park Authority. However most of it is privately owned, a massive 25 per cent of the park's landscape being protected land owned by the National Trust, with a mere 4 per cent owned by the National Park Authority.

On a practical level there is now a sudden reduction in the number of dedicated Cumbria Way signs, since the National Park Authority is unfortunately under no obligation to indicate unofficial long distance routes. The occasional Cumbria Way sign can be spotted in the National Park but essentially walkers must use ordinary public footpath signs.

Leaving Gawthwaite behind, the route continues down a small country lane to a gate and a stile, together with a sign indicating that this stretch of the Way is shared with an official off-road route for motorised vehicles. The use of such vehicles within the boundaries of a National Park has become, and continues to be, a cause of great controversy. There are numerous arguments for and against their use, although the general opinion is that they are here to stay. With many modern farmers using 4-wheel drive quad bikes, perhaps it must simply be accepted that motorised vehicles are now part of modern-day Cumbria life.

To the north-east are the first views of Coniston Water, and on a clear day the distant Langdale Pikes. The track passes the small settlement at High Stennerley, before continuing shortly along a small country lane and heading right into another field. The route starts to become a little sketchy at this point, but a good rule of thumb is to follow closely the wire fence, keeping to the left of it and passing the first opening until you reach a more defined clearing on the right. At this point walkers should enter the adjacent field and branch again towards the right, where there is a somewhat rustic plastic arrow indicating the route. Now the route becomes simpler as it heads towards the wall at the bottom of the field and then over a stile built into the high dry stone wall and leading to the next stretch of the way.

Once again the route now follows a small country lane until it reaches the turn off for Kiln Bank farm. In this area it is possible to catch a glimpse of the common buzzard, preying on small rats, voles and rabbits. Hawks and other birds of prey are a common sight in the Lakes, with the rich natural landscape providing a perfect habitat for both predator and prey.

Next the Cumbria Way follows the track towards Kiln Bank, eventually turning right at the farmhouse where Cumbria Way signs direct walkers along a well-defined farm track. Crossing a wooden ladder stile over a dry stone wall the trail continues briefly uphill via a country lane before taking a well-defined route to the right into a landscape that is in stark contrast to the preceding stretch.

The route now passes through moorland which is barren for much of the year but is covered in high summer by the greens of native foliage and a radiant carpet of purple flowers. On reaching the brow of the hill, the impressive form of Beacon Tarn soon becomes visible. If weather conditions are favourable, the tarn will act as a natural mirror, with the reflections of the surrounding landscape in the water accentuating the already beautiful scenery. Heading towards the tarn and veering left at the water's edge, the Way follows a small but well-defined path formed by the feet of walkers past. This area is truly tranquil and is a good place if time allows to take a lunch or snack break and enjoy the peace and serenity that it has to offer.

Tarns are a glacial by-product. As huge lumps of ice scoured and carved this remarkable landscape, deposits of compacted ice were occasionally split off the main body of the glacier. These lumps of ice then melted into depressions forming small glacial lakes (or tarns as they are known locally), which are now found scattered throughout the fells of the Lake District.

This untamed landscape reinforces the necessity for a good map and compass. The route now begins to descend, and on a fine day there are commanding views of the Old Man of Coniston as well as the highest mountain in England, Scafell Pike at 3164 feet. Throughout this section of the Way the ground underfoot is particularly boggy and slippery even in fine weather, so care should be taken when negotiating the descent through a valley surrounded by smoothly undulating, fern covered hills.

Eventually the walker will see a stone house and a lane in the far distance which serve as a guide to the direction that should now be taken. The Way heads towards this lane and then briefly along a stretch of tarmac, before branching along a public bridleway roughly following the small electricity pylons that supply the small settlements in the area. Soon the bridleway reaches a small tarn which is another fine example of the Lake District's glacial past. From here the route continues towards the distant form of Coniston Water, keeping close to the banks of Mere Beck. On reaching the Torver Beck and crossing the small wooden bridge spanning across this beautiful, fast-flowing stream which is a perfect location to spot dragonflies in the summer months, the track follows the nearby wall until it arrives at a small road. After crossing the road the trail continues across the open moorland of Torver Common and finally reaches the lakeside of Coniston Water.

In complete contrast to the yachts and steamers that now frequent peaceful Coniston Water, several world water speed records were set here. Sir Malcolm Campbell was the first to throw the spotlight onto the third largest of the Lake District's waters, the five-mile long lake providing perfect conditions for him to set the world water speed record on 19th August 1939 of 141.74 miles per hour. His record-breaking boat, the Bluebird K4, was used for further record attempts by his son, Donald Campbell, but it was not to be this vessel that further placed the Campbell name in the history books. The K4 was destroyed in a crash at 156 miles per hour and Donald Campbell began developing a new boat.

The Bluebird K7 was a jet propelled hydroplane vessel which worked on the principle of skimming the water rather than ploughing through it. This enabled Campbell to set four new world water speed records between the years of 1956 and 1959. By 1966 he had decided that the three hundred miles per hour limit had to be exceeded, leading the way to another world record attempt at Coniston on 4th January 1967.

This fateful winter's day was to see Campbell achieve a first run of 297 miles per hour. He quickly took the rash decision to not refuel his boat and began his second run. This aimed to smash the world record and break the 300 miles per hour barrier. Unfortunately, his haste to start the second run so quickly meant that the wake on the lake was still unsettled from his first run, and the lack of refuelling meant that the K7 was lighter and less stable. This second run was to end in disaster, with the K7 being catapulted into the sky, somersaulting and crashing nose down onto the lake before sinking into the murky depths below. This was to be the last resting place of Donald Campbell until a controversial decision was taken to recover the remains of him and his boat in 2001.

The Way now starts to follow the banks of the lake as it meanders through the contrasting moorland and forest landscapes of neighbouring Torver Common. The track passes a jetty for steamers until it reaches a campsite, then a further small jetty beside a larger campsite. This National Trust campsite makes a great spot for an overnight stay, with the possibility of viewing early morning mists rising from the lake for those willing to peel themselves out of their sleeping bags early in the morning.

The weak early morning sun highlights features of the undulating hills surrounding Ulverston.

A brief stretch of the track joining a quiet country lane ablaze with the colours of summer foliage.

Nasturtium and other flowers growing next to a Cumbria Way sign near the Lake District National Park Boundary at Gawthwaite.

A native fern growing beside a typical Lakeland dry stone wall.

Female hiker walking a stretch of the track from High Stennerley to Kendall Ground.

The Cumbria Way track following the road from Kendall ground to Kiln Bank.

A small beck flowing through farmland near Kiln Bank Farm.

A ladder stile offers hikers a helping step over a dry stone wall near Tottlebank.

The route continues through fields and farmland near Tottlebank.

Dusk as hikers wild camp next to the shore of Beacon Tarn.

The autumn hues of Beacon Fell, looking towards Torver Common.

Power lines carry electricity across the remote landscape of Torver Common.

A small tarn on Torver Low Common.

A wooden bridge allowing hikers to safely pass across the fast rapids of Torver Beck.

A moored boat reflected in the still waters of Coniston Water at dawn in mid summer.

Dawn looking across the tranquil waters of Coniston Water.

A blanket of ferns growing in Torver Common Wood.

Lakeland houses in Conistion against an impressive mountainous backdrop.

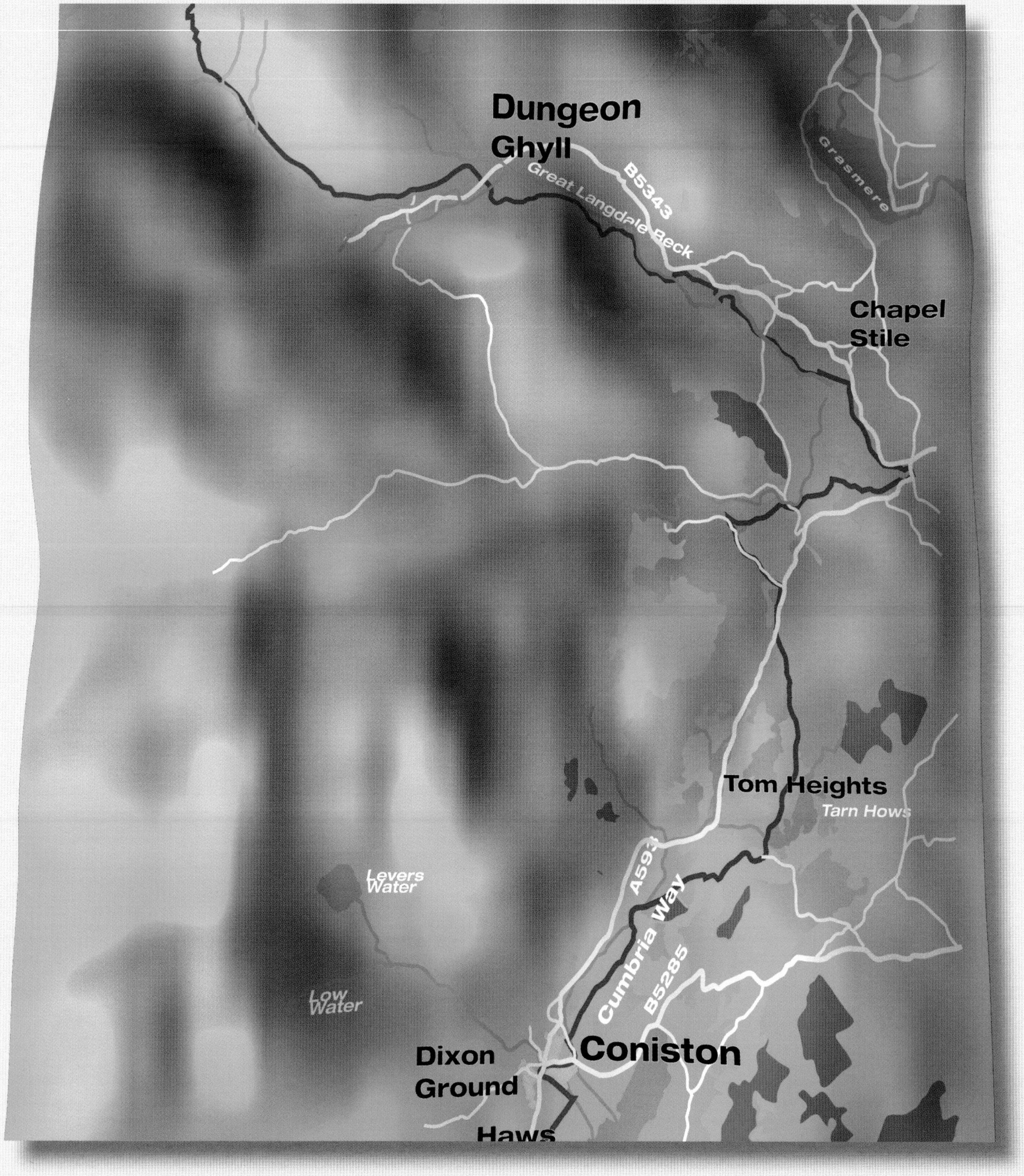
Dungeon
Ghyll
Great Langdale Beck
B5343
Grasmere
Chapel
Stile
Tom Heights
Tarn Hows
Levers
Water
A593
Cumbria Way
B5285
Low
Water
Dixon
Ground
Coniston
Haws

Coniston to Dungeon Ghyll

The day ahead provides an excellent opportunity to discover many of the qualities that led to this area being designated a National Park. A good night's sleep and hearty food are always required by the walker undertaking a multi-day hike, and Coniston is always a great location for a traditional full English breakfast – believe me, I've had my share!

The Way now continues along Tilberthwaite Avenue before taking a left turn down a quiet lane. After a short stroll a stone bridge appears on the right, leading across Yewdale Beck. Turn immediately left at the stile and follow the public footpath as it gently begins to climb through farmland to a rustic stone building from where you continue onwards towards the woods in the distance. Here the Way follows a small track through the trees before joining a forestry commission vehicle track used to access pockets of woodland which are felled on a rotational basis. A brief uphill route, sandwiched between fields and trees, allows fine views towards the mountains and fells to the west. The path passes Tarn Hows Cottage – a typical Lakeland-style habitation – then takes a small track to Tarn Hows Road, which should be followed to the left. By now it is possible to appreciate the height gained since leaving Coniston, rewarding you with a panorama of upland views as you continue onwards to one of the most scenic spots to be found along the entire Way.

The Tarn Hows of today is drastically different from the one that would have been seen more than two hundred years ago. This peaceful and picturesque tarn was once three separate tarns before these were joined to form a single stretch of water. It is in fact something of a man-made feature, the plantation of conifers surrounding the banks once again being one product of human interference, although this does not mean in any way that the Tarn is less picturesque than any other of the Lake District's natural attractions.

Beatrix Potter had strong connections with the Lake District and played an active role in its conservation. The famous illustrator and writer, who came originally from London, frequently holidayed in the area before and after her first children's book 'The Tale of Peter Rabbit' was published in 1902. It was Derwentwater that was to provide the backdrop for her third book, 'The Tale of Squirrel Nutkin'. Soon she was living and working in Cumbria where she eventually purchased the Monk Coniston Estate, which included Tarn Hows. She later sold Tarn Hows and nearly half of the estate to the National Trust, leading to the preservation of a landscape to be enjoyed by many past, present and future generations of Beatrix Potter fans as well as Cumbria Way walkers.

The route continues along the well-defined track to the left of the Tarn and through woodland, before reaching a junction and a track to the left. After a brief while along this easy to navigate section, the walker will find themselves in a slightly elevated upland area in which impressive views of the surrounding scenery are almost guaranteed, before eventually reaching a small country lane leading to reach a larger and somewhat busier road. At this point the route crosses the road and follows the impressive stone walls to the right through farmland until reaching a ladder stile. Here the Way follows the road signposted 'High Park'. Continue along until just before reaching High Park Farm, then enter a field through the gate and head along the way-marked route to the neighbouring woods.

This delightful pocket of deciduous woodland is home to wild deer and if the wind is in a favourable direction, a quiet hiker, may be granted a glimpse of these magnificent animals. The route now carries on through woodland offering a choice of two routes. The official route continues along the well-defined track through this picturesque woodland, whereas the second branches off to the left and the serene Colwith Force – a testament to the sculpting effects of water upon the landscape of the Lake District. Both routes eventually lead to a road near Colwith Bridge. Crossing the road and entering the small field via a stile built into the wall, the Way heads towards another pocket of woodland, which is transformed into a riot of colour during late autumn.

By now the track is starting to climb gently through the trees. These once again give way to fields where the track continues to meander through farmland until reaching the busy Coniston-Ambleside Road, at which point it follows the road towards Skelwith Bridge, where it crosses over a quaint bridge and heads left, loosely following the direction of the River Brathay via the public footpath that cuts through the slate workshops. Here there is a café which is a great place to have a cuppa overlooking the river. The trail shortly reaches Skelwith Force – a raging course of water after heavy rain. Continue along the track to the point where the river begins to enlarge as it merges into Elterwater, which is a deceivingly unrecognisable lake unless viewed from the hilltops above. This is a very serene spot and visitors to Elterwater on a calm day may view the reflections of mature neighbouring trees in the still waters of the lake. In spring the surrounding woodland is transformed by a thick blanket of native bluebells splashing colour into this already vibrant landscape.

The route now officially continues via the fields immediately in front. However another option at this point is to keep to the well-defined track along the banks of Elterwater until the path begins to follow a small beck, and the official Cumbria Way route once again continues onwards. After passing through a small gate onto a country road through the tiny village of Elterwater, the Way follows the beck upstream (it is important to take care on the road past the mines, as it is often used by industrial vehicles transporting slate quarried from the area), and eventually reaches a small bridge, where it crosses over into the village of Chapel Stile.

Chapel Stile is the location of a public house named after one of Cumbria's most famous fell walkers – Alfred Wainwright. Wainwright's love of the Lakeland fells is well documented through his series 'Pictorial Guides to the Lakeland Fells', for which he researched and visited more than two hundred fells. With their hand-drawn sketches, his guides inspire fell walkers to this day. Wainwright also wrote various other books based on Cumbria and the north of England in general. Perhaps his most famous legacy was designing the Coast to Coast walk, a 190 mile long track running from St Bees Head in Cumbria to Robin Hood's Bay in North Yorkshire.

The Cumbria Way passes behind the inn, continuing through a small settlement of houses towards the farm campsite and once again crosses over the beck. By now the beck has gradually started to increase in size and to deserve its title of the Great Langdale Beck. The Way now follows loosely the path of the beck, occasionally straying away from the banks to climb high above it before dropping down alongside it. The landscape here is a spectacular panorama of Lakeland mountain views, with fern-covered fells, watercourses and rocky outcrops all in view until one reaches the inn at Dungeon Ghyll and a well deserved rest after completing the second leg of the route.

An old Oak Tree standing proud alongside the route of the Cumbria Way near Tarn Hows Wood.

Storm clouds clear from high above the picturesque Tarn Hows.

The autumnal colours of the landscape near Holme Fell.

Flowering Fox Gloves within a pocket of woodland near High Oxen Fell.

The River Brathy flowing through the green expanse of Colwith Woods.

The river downstream of Skelwith Force, near the small village of Skelwith Bridge.

A close up view of a native bluebell photographed in woodland by Elterwater.

The surrounding fell side and vegetation reflected in the still waters of Elterwater.

The route continues over an old stone bridge near Elterwater village.

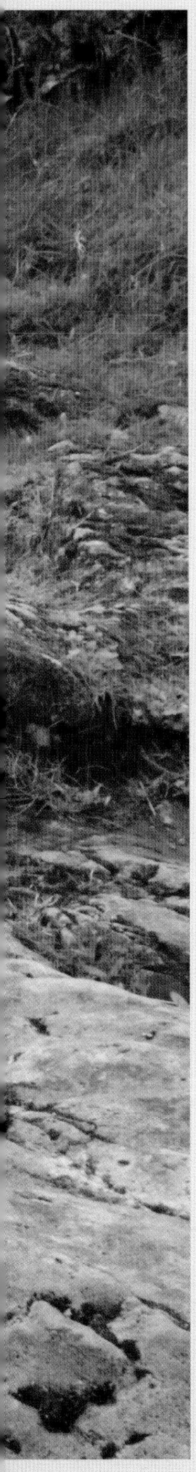

Flowing rapids continue to carve the moss engulfed rocks.

The Great Langdale Beck running through woodland near Chapel Stile.

The flowing waterfalls of Dungeon Ghyll Force, near Langdale Fell.

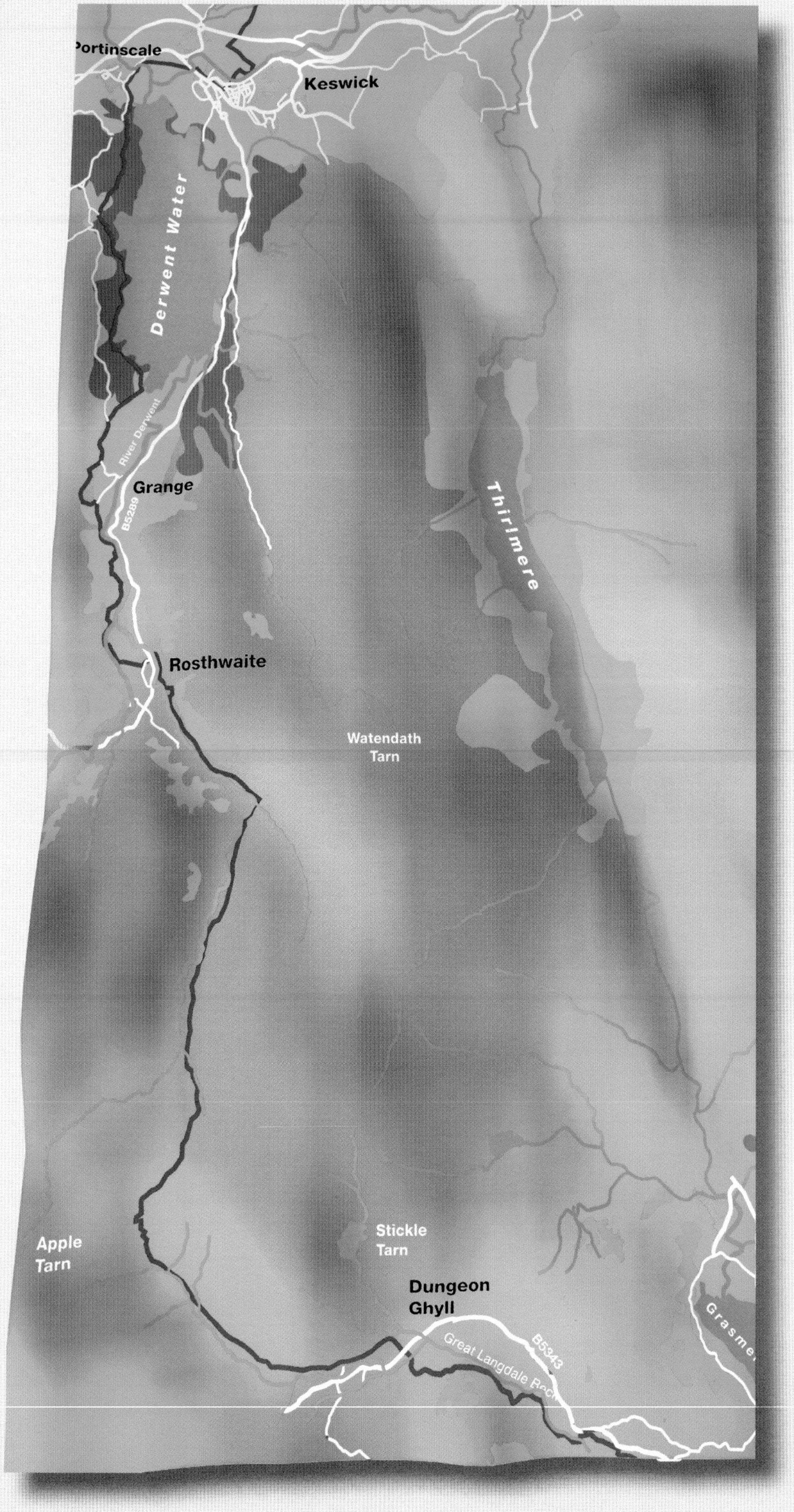
Portinscale
Keswick
Derwent Water
River Derwent
Grange
B5289
Thirlmere
Rosthwaite
Watendlath
Tarn
Apple
Tarn
Stickle
Tarn
Dungeon
Ghyll
B5343
Great Langdale Road
Grasmere

Dungeon Ghyll to Keswick

The starting point for the third day of the route will depend on one's choice of accommodation the previous night. Walkers desiring creature comforts will probably have stayed near, or indeed at the New Dungeon Ghyll Hotel and will simply need to take the track running to the west of the inn to rejoin the trail. Campers will rejoin the track at the Old Dungeon Ghyll Hotel, approximately 1 mile west of the new hotel.

An early start during the autumn months may provide the opportunity to observe mists lifting from the valley as the weak, early morning sun begins to warm the crisp dawn air. The actual route involves a short but sharp incline towards the Dungeon Ghyll falls, before branching to the left and following a slightly elevated path in the valley through farmland used for grazing sheep. As the Way passes the Old Dungeon Ghyll Hotel (a wonderfully charismatic public house for a spot of food and a pint of beer - as you may have discovered the night before, if camping). It then levels out as it goes down the Langdale valley following the Mickelden stream as views of mountainous peaks unfold.

The Langdale Valley is a true glacial landscape with its distinctive U-shaped valley and craggy features carved by vast amounts of compacted ice. This area has had a turbulent natural history with evidence of both volcanic eruptions and glacial activity.

Along Mickleden it is flat easy walking, where you are likely to see sheep grazing on the lower levels and often towards the tops during the summer months. The following stage of the Way is one of the most arduous, although the hard work will reap its rewards. On reaching a small wooden bridge at the end of the valley there is a beck on your right and a boulder painted which is with a crude arrow and the inscription 'Stake Pass'. It is necessary to follow the directions and to keep initially near to Stake Gill before the route becomes more defined. There is now a network of many routes heading towards the top of Stake Pass but walkers must continue along the well-defined official route of the Way, not one of the many short cuts created by people trying to 'cut corners'. Now it is time for a steady, gradual ascent up to the pass. The views back towards Mickleden are impressive and improve with every step. Climbing upwards, the mountains seem to unfold, revealing the true glory of their peaks that can only be fully appreciated from a viewpoint of near equivalent height. It has been suggested that the Cumbria Way would make a better route if walked in the reverse direction, and if there are any exceptional grounds for this argument then Stake Pass and Stake Gill are it.

As always seems to be the case, on reaching what you expect to be the top of the pass, you discover a new landscape and that the path continues further uphill! After one last steep ascent it becomes a steady route towards the top of Stake Pass (1576 ft).

It has been suggested that the open fell at the top of the pass is a bleak and inhospitable place. Sit down and allow time to let the world go by and you will most probably be quite surprised by the variety of wildlife that makes its home in this landscape. Amazingly, there is evidence that this open, wild land was also once a home for Homo sapiens during the Neolithic period. Now there are definitely no signs of human habitation although it does attract many keen hikers and climbers.

The route roughly follows the Stake Beck until the imposing presence of the Langstrath and the Langstrath valley below provide magnificent views along this wild stretch of the Cumbria Way.

At this stage walkers cross an important watershed where the gently flowing waters of the Stake Beck start their journey to become part of the River Derwent and eventually join the Solway Firth towards the Scottish Borders. Up until this point, all the water headed south towards Morecambe Bay. This is effectively the middle point of the Cumbria Way (although it may be worth holding off celebrations until you have climbed its highest point!).

On reaching the foot of the pass and after crossing a small bridge, the Way continues to the right of the beck as you begin a gentle hike through the largest uninhabited valley in England. Personally I regard this as one of the most tranquil stretches of the Cumbria Way, and one that receives far less human traffic than other areas but still boasts a landscape that must truly be considered one of the most spectacular in England, if not the British Isles. The route meanders through the valley for about two miles before the beck eventually makes a sharp turn to the left as its waters begin to merge with the Greenup Gill and form Stonethwaite Beck.

From here it continues onwards keeping the now larger beck to the left. The path shortly passes a National Trust campsite which can be seen on the other side of the beck. This is a wonderfully rustic campsite which is a good spot to pitch a tent at any time of the year. I wholeheartedly recommend that if you can spare the time, plan to spend a night here and break up this stretch of the route, as it is the most arduous but also possibly the most enjoyable. What could be better than enjoying a brew in your camp near the banks of the beck, followed by a well deserved pint in the local tavern?

The Cumbria Way continues alongside the beck following a well-defined track sandwiched between some particularly fine examples of dry stone walling. It is quite possible that these walls have stood for many generations, being repaired as necessary using the same painstaking techniques as when the walls were originally built. There is an art to dry stone walling which luckily has not been lost with the introduction of modern farming techniques. In fact, landowners are often required to maintain the appearance of walls to preserve the character of the area.

At the end of the track a sign indicates a route to a bunk house, which is another option for overnight accommodation should you wish to break up this stage. Branching left across a stone bridge until reaching a small road, the route heads left and then takes the first immediate right, continuing past a few houses and through a farmyard until it merges into a farm track. Eventually the Way joins the course of the River Derwent and follows its banks past a group of stepping stones until it arrives at a small, typical Lakeland stone bridge, whereupon it crosses this 'New Bridge' and follows a well-defined track.

Before long the Way enters what is arguably one of the finest examples of woodland found anywhere in the National Park. During autumn it is often possible to find numerous varieties of fungi, growing on both living and dead hosts. It would be easy to assume that fungi are simply parasites which attach themselves to a host, but this is not always the case. In many cases fungi actually extend the tree's root system, improving the uptake of water and nutrients. Fungi also provide great support for numerous animals and insects, with over a thousand species being dependent on fungi for shelter and food in the UK alone. If you do plan to search for fungi, it should be remembered that a few examples of highly poisonous species can be found.

The Way now traverses woodland along a track that passes through the open remnants of slate quarrying and the occasional cave, again a reminder of the area's slate quarrying past. Next the route rejoins the river and passes a small, picturesque rustic National Trust campsite, hidden amongst oak trees against a classic fell backdrop. Although this site can often be busy at weekends and Bank Holidays, it is quite possible that outside these periods you may find you are the only soul present.

After leaving the river the Way heads along a small bridleway until reaching a lane where it veers left towards Hollows Farm. It then passes through the farmyard and through a gate, before continuing along a bridleway towards the Grange. By now the mountains have begun to display characteristics that differ distinctly from the previous examples of craggy peaks formed from the hard Borrowdale rock of volcanic origin. The mountainous landscape that lies ahead is made from a softer material, Skiddaw Slate, which consequently has created mountains of a gentle, smoother appearance.

After going right through a farm gate into the Grange, walkers are rewarded with their first views of Derwent Water, undeniably one of the most popular lakes. Here, a small bench situated on a grassy bank provides a welcome spot to take the strain off your legs, and an opportunity simply to admire the views of the lake and, if the weather is good, the distant slopes of Skiddaw. This is the first chance to view the eventual path of the next leg of the Way.

The route now heads through farmland, before turning left onto a small country road then branching right through a meadow, which has a colourful abundance of wild flowers in spring. There follows a stretch of woodland before the shores of the lake are reached. It is worth savouring this expanse of flatness – your legs will welcome the easy pace of this section of the Way after the steep climb and descent of the previous stages. There are numerous signposts for Keswick before you eventually leave the lake along small country lanes and public footpaths and finally reach the town.

A fleeting shaft of light illuminates the rustic features of the Langdale mountains.

A small beck amidst the red hues of the wild landscape encountered on the Cumbria Way as it heads towards Stake Pass.

A hiker looks at the impressive wild scenery of the Mickleden Valley.

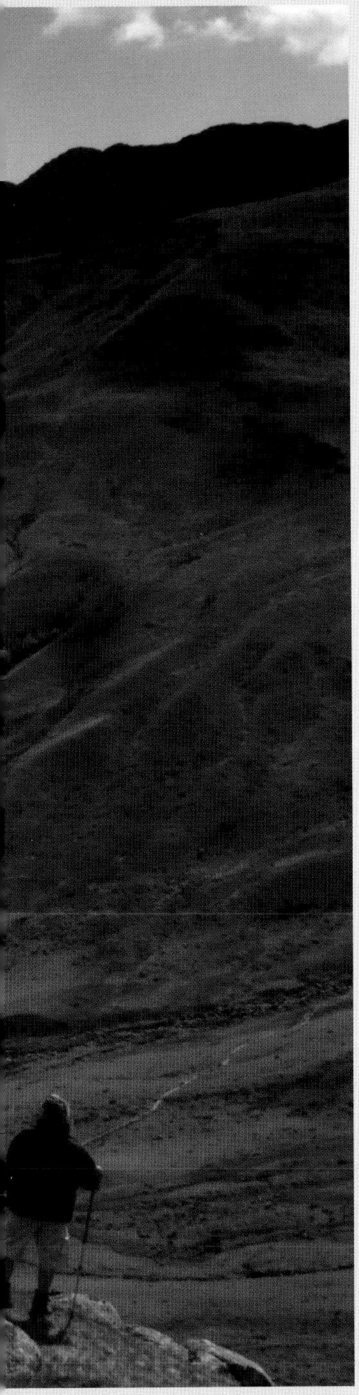

Late afternoon light illuminates the lichen covered rocks of Martcrag Moor.

Brief shafts of sun illuminate the surrounding peaks of the Langstrath Valley.

Gallen Force near Stonethwaite, continues to erode and carve the natural rocks creating a small gorge.

The track between Stonethwaite and Rosthwaite runs between an impressive stretch of dry stone walling built over a metre high.

The Cumbria Way route passes over 'New Bridge' crossing the river Derwent in Borrowdale.

Borrowdale Valley, looking towards Stonethwaite Beck and the Langstrath Valley.

Bracket fungus photographed on a dead birch tree in woodland near Borrowdale.

A disused quarry near to the route of the Cumbria Way track as it heads through Dalt Wood.

Borrowdale mountains reflected in the still waters of the River Derwent.

A gentle stream flowing through Dalt Wood during autumn.

The Cumbria Way now joins a quiet road heading towards Hollows Farm.

Woodland found close to the banks of Derwent Water.

View overlooking Derwentwater towards the country's fourth highest mountain - Skiddaw.

The surrounding autumn colours of woodland and mountain backdrop, reflected in the still waters of Derwentwater.

Flowering hawthorne tree bush in a hedgerow near Derwentwater.

Keswick to Caldbeck

The picturesque town of Keswick has an extensive history that dates back to the Neolithic period. The nearby Castlerigg Stone Circle is a fine example of what is probably one of the earliest stone circles built in the British Isles. With an estimated construction date of around 3000 BC, its well-preserved remains make a rewarding diversion, as well as providing good views of the route ahead, which heads north through some of the most barren landscape to be found along the entire Way.

More recently Keswick, like many other Lakeland towns, has became famous for its regular Saturday market. However it is the cheese fairs which were held frequently until the 1900s that have left a lasting mark on the town. The old English name for Keswick was 'Cese-wic' which translates loosely as 'cheese town'. The discovery of graphite in nearby Borrowdale and the abundant local supply of timber has led Keswick to become a major manufacturing area for the humble pencil, and at the local pencil museum the largest pencil in the world is on display.

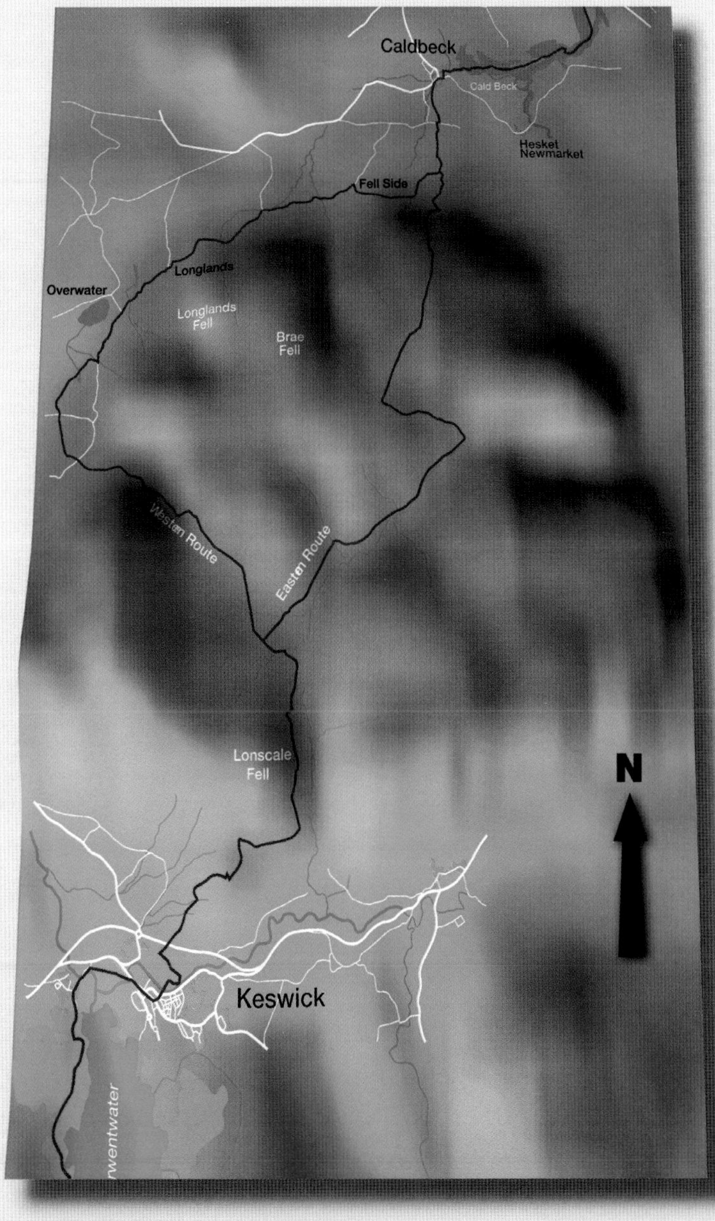

Hikers continuing beyond Keswick should prepare themselves for what can be one of the most arduous stages of the walk, with the prospect of climbing the final and also highest mountain pass of the entire Way. Keswick offers numerous shops for stocking up with food and fuel, and there is certainly no shortage of pubs! This stretch of the route differs from the others since it has an alternative route designated for days of poor visibility. However I recommend that if you find yourself about to embark on this stage in unfavourable weather conditions, take the opportunity (if time allows) of having a rest day in Keswick and wait hopefully for the weather to improve. The rewards from a day spent 'taking it easy' will soon become apparent when proceeding along the high level route.

The Cumbria Way skirts through the town, crossing the River Greta shortly before passing around Keswick's swimming pool and leisure centre (extremely popular with both visitors and locals on Lakeland's typically rainy days). It now proceeds past a disused railway, then continues briefly along a fairly quiet country road before heading north across a bridge over the busy and controversial bypass. Spooney Green Lane is a return to tranquillity with its mixture of broad-leaved woodland and fine views back towards the town and the surrounding mountains. As the Way continues steadily onwards and upwards, good views of the Latrigg summit can be enjoyed as you skirt the edges of woodland, until the dominating form of Skiddaw and the surrounding vastness of wild moorland come into sight. On joining the road, the route heads east until shortly arriving at a small car park, from where it continues north until it reaches the small Hawell monument, which is dedicated to the memory of three Lonscale shepherds. Leaving behind the views of Skiddaw it now continues east across White Beck towards what is possibly one of the last remaining wildernesses in England.

When walking along this well-defined track, it is worth taking the time to look back towards the town and Derwentwater, with good views of the route as it follows the valley of Borrowdale. In spring and autumn walkers may be rewarded with picture postcard views of mist rising from the crisp waters of Derwentwater and engulfing the surrounding hillsides to create an enchanting spectacle. From this point the Way starts to acquire a different feel, and as it heads onwards towards Blencathra the route slowly follows the lower reaches of Lonscale Fell high above the Glenderaterra Beck. From here onwards the landscape is distinctly different from what was encountered previously. The route is still well-defined but it can be difficult to traverse during or after periods of high rainfall. In summer the landscape and its undulating hills become a colourful array of purple heather and green ferns, with the silence of the hills being briefly broken by the rustle of birds flying out of the dense heather. You will soon realise that this stage of the route receives far less attention from hikers and tourists than the earlier stretches of the Way which lie closer to the heart of the National Park. Tranquillity may prevail for the next few miles if the weather conditions are on your side, with hiker and landscape becoming one as the route continues gently towards the north. However days like these are few and far between, and when you reach the youth hostel at Skiddaw House, it will be time to make an important decision regarding your route and possibly safety.

As previously mentioned, the Cumbria Way now divides into two different routes. If visibility is good and the mountain tops and hills can be easily viewed towards the north east, you can continue along the eastern route of the Way, branching right from the track towards the distant valley formed by the River Caldrew. However if visibility is poor it is advisable to continue along the original track past Skiddaw House towards Candleseaves Bog and the Whitewater Dash waterfall. For the purposes of this book it has been decided that details will only be given for the high level route.

Skiddaw House, situated at a height of 1550 feet, is the highest youth hostel in Britain. Originally built as a shooting lodge in the early 20th Century, it later became a shepherd's bothy before finally being abandoned and subsequently vandalised in the late 1950s. Located in the shadow of Skiddaw, England's fourth highest mountain, it was donated to the Youth Hostel Association (YHA) on the understanding that they would manage its upkeep and return it to its former splendour. Now complete with a resident warden, Skiddaw House makes an ideal place to rest your head for the night for anyone wishing to break up this stage of the journey.

Walkers who are fortunate to have good visibility will be able to take the high level route, which branches right from Skiddaw House and follows a well-defined track before reaching a small footbridge across the River Caldrew, which begins its course on the slopes of nearby Skiddaw. Although now in the heart of a truly wild landscape, you can enjoy the next few miles walking on even terrain, loosely following the route of the Caldrew as it begins its journey to the heart of industrial Carlisle, carving through the undulating hills to create a vista of mountain and sky.

Shortly after crossing a bridge over Grainsgill Beck, the Way branches to the left towards the disused Carrock Mine. This is an area which is extremely rich in minerals and has been mined since the early 13th Century. Tungsten, iron, copper and zinc have been found here, together with more than 150 other different minerals, fuelling something of a flurry in the mining industry in the 17th Century. Mining ceased on the Caldbeck fells in the 1960s but its legacy remains, so it is important to keep as close to the defined route as possible over the next few miles. The familiar exhortation to 'leave only footprints and take only pictures' is particularly appropriate here and is reinforced by National Park signs throughout the area reminding you to let nature be.

At this point the route becomes less defined, following the Grainsgill beck upstream until the path begins to level out. Here it is possible to see in the distance a small wooden building which you should head towards, following the now well-defined track until you reach Lingy Hut. Named after the nearby Great Lingy Hill, this began life as a simple shooting box. It is now in the hands of the Lake District National Park and is provided as a simple mountain shelter for anyone who may require emergency protection in poor weather and nil visibility. However it is not a large or luxurious property and should not be relied upon. Anyone planning to spend the night up the hills would find a tent a far better option (but don't forget to get the landowner's permission first).

Leaving Lingy Hut the trail continues towards High Pike and is rewarded by spectacular vistas. From the cairn at High Pike, at 2159 feet the highest point of the Cumbria Way, there are 360° views as far as the eye can see, with a glimpse of what the next stages of the Way have to offer. Walkers are often at the mercy of the elements, with unrelenting winds causing difficulties on even the finest day. However this always makes a nice break for a snack, hopefully allowing time to admire the last views of the heart of the National Park, as well as the Scottish Borders to the north. From here the route starts to descend and the landscape that has dominated the last two days of the walk is finally left behind.

Descending from High Peak, you pass more disused mine shafts towards the hamlet of Nether Row, traversing the grassy slopes of the fell side before eventually meeting a well-defined track to the hamlet, from where a combination of country lanes and brief stretches of public footpath lead to the 13th century village of Caldbeck and a well deserved meal and a pint!

Castlerigg stone circle at dusk.

Looking towards Keswick and the backdrop of Skiddaw.

A hiker enjoys a viewpoint near Ewe How.

Whit Beck, surrounded by a light dusting of winter snow.

View from Lower Lonscale, looking across fields near the town of Keswick.

Snow along the well formed track as it continues towards Caldbeck.

Summer ferns on the slopes of the valley between Lonscale and Blease Fell.

A female hiker climbs a stile along the track near Lonscale Fell.

The vibrant colours of flowering heather found during the height of summer.

Salehow Beck amidst purple flowering heather near Skiddaw House.

View looking along the Cumbria Way track running from Skiddaw House towards Caldbeck.

A lonely tree on the barren landscape of Caldbeck Common.

Grainsgill Beck running down the moorland of Lingy Hill.

The soft hues of the setting sun illuminate Lingy Hut on Caldbeck Common.

A cairn on High Pike marks the highest point of the Cumbria Way track (658m).

A hiker enjoys a break admiring the scenery from the slopes of High Peak.

Looking towards the hamlet of Nether Row.

The well defined track shortly before reaching Nether Row.

After the hamlet of Nether Row, the route continues along quiet country lanes until it reaches Caldbeck.

The gentle flow of the Cald Beck, running through Caldbeck village.

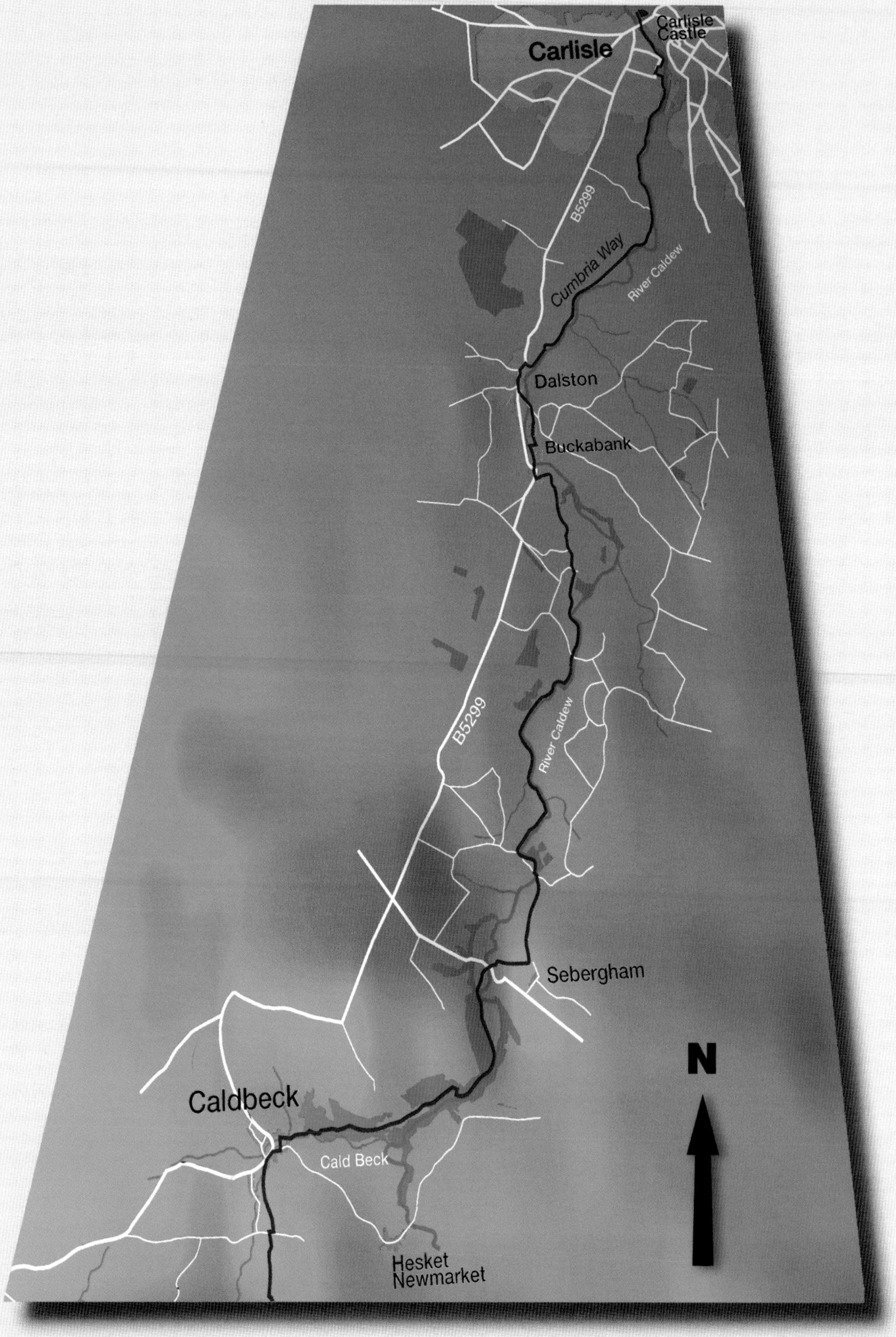
Carlisle
Carlisle Castle
B5299
Cumbria Way
River Caldew
Dalston
Buckabank
B5299
River Caldew
Sebergham
N
Caldbeck
Cald Beck
Hesket Newmarket

Caldbeck to Carlisle

The landscape along the route from Caldbeck to Carlisle may not be as spectacular as the previous four stages, but it has its own charm nevertheless. Cumbria is an incredibly beautiful county and although most people associate it with mountains and lakes, the countryside found here echoes the stereotypical view of the great English outdoors. Maybe Caldbeck is the classic English village?

Cumbria has many different traditions from the rest of the country and fox hunting is no exception, with its history of hunts being conducted on foot by local fell farmers as a means of defending their livestock. It has been said that one Wasdale farmer alone lost more than 50 lambs in one season owing to attacks by foxes. In January 2005 this tradition became only history when legislation was passed to ban fox hunting, although the arguments and lobbying from those in favour of hunting will continue to be voiced for many years after the ban and in some instances it may be difficult initially to enforce the legislation.

Caldbeck Church, dating from the 12th Century, and the summer colours of the surrounding gardens.

Caldbeck's most famous son is one of England's most infamous huntsmen. John Peel was born in Caldbeck in 1776. One of a family of thirteen children, he grew up to become something of an enigma in the hunting world and eventually formed his own hunting pack. He led a colourful life, eloping to Gretna Green to marry his sweetheart immediately after her mother forbad their wedding in Caldbeck church because she felt that they were too young. John Peel was immortalised in the 18th century ballad (and later tune), 'D'ye Ken John Peel?' Upon his death in 1854, over 3000 huntsmen attended his funeral at Caldbeck Church to pay their respects to one of the most effective and successful fox hunters of all time.

It is near John Peel's resting spot that the Cumbria Way begins its final journey north. Passing beside the picturesque church and across a small stone bridge over the beck before heading down towards a sewage works, walkers should be sure to look back at the great expanse of hills that they traversed the day before.

Quickly skirting the sewage works before arriving at a small wooden gate, a track leads down to Parsons Park Wood. After the extensive storms in the early part of 2005 this stretch was virtually impassable. Although this may appear to be natural destruction on a colossal scale, it should be remembered that this is a natural ongoing process which has happened throughout the millennia and will continue to do so. There has been talk of freak weather patterns with the topical issue of global warming, but maybe in reality we are just witnessing something of a natural cycle. Cumbria is renowned for fickle weather so it is of little surprise that extreme effects of weather should affect the landscape.

Continuing onwards, the route passes through a pocket of deciduous woodland before branching down a forestry commission track into the mixed pine and birch of Dentonside Wood. Here the trail meets the River Caldrew, which it follows closely for the remainder of the route to Carlisle.

The track must be followed until it reaches the road at Sebergham Bridge, where care is needed both crossing the bridge and road before heading to the left through a small gate and heading gradually uphill towards the church. On leaving the river and climbing a height, it is possible to enjoy the views of the Caldrew running through the valley and surrounding fells. Continuing along the track the route passes Sebergham Hall before dropping back down to river level and rejoining the route of the River Caldrew at Bell Bridge.

The next few miles are a gentle stroll through farmland and fields keeping to the banks of the River Caldew, although for those who have walked the complete route with a tent and back pack it may feel a little more arduous! This stretch provides a perfect habitat for what seems like the majority of the Cumbrian Sheep tick population, especially during the summer months. Anyone who finds that they have become the object of unwanted attention from one of these pests will find it is a relatively simple process to remove them. A pair of tweezers should be used to carefully remove them from the skin by pulling the creature from as near to the head as possible, taking care not to rupture the body of the tick in order to avoid any unwanted infection. It is advisable to check every part of your body after walking through a tick infected area and if you are in any doubt as to whether the entire tick has been successfully removed, you should seek medical attention.

This stretch of the track makes a wonderful way to pass a few hours on a sunny afternoon. Continue along past Bell Bridge before you finally come to Rose Bridge and an unbelievable tight squeeze through two metal gates. One feature that will have become apparent by now is the abundance of Cumbria Way signs.

After Rose Bridge you continue beside the river for approximately 500 yards before branching away to the left through fields before passing the grounds of Lime House School and then shortly afterwards Holmhill Farm. The route now goes slightly uphill through farmland. Looking back at the route you have just come, there is a diminishing view of the Cumbrian hills and mountains. From this point they will be but distant memories as you progress through fields before eventually reaching Bridge End. The route now follows the road through the small village of Buckabank, before crossing the river and entering the town of Dalston.

This small town, with its somewhat unique motto of 'where I live I crow', shows obvious signs of an industrial heritage, which is not entirely surprising considering that the first cotton mill was established here in 1780 and that you are now only just over four miles from your final destination of Carlisle. The industry now based around Dalston is something of a mixed bag, ranging from a saw, corn and cotton mill to the dominating presence of the Nestle factory. However they all share one common natural resource – the water power of the River Caldew.

This final stretch of the Way continues along the river, sharing the route with a cycle path. By now the path is well formed and level, although the tarmac will start to take its toll on weary feet!

The last few miles of the Cumbria Way are subject to change. The Ramblers Association has long been looking to improve the final couple of miles of the Way, but decisions relating to the route are not entirely within its control.

The start of January 2005 saw a torrential downfall on the city of Carlisle equivalent to a month's normal rainfall. Coupled with gale force winds of up to 100 miles per hour, Carlisle was ravaged by possibly the worst storm in living history and eventually three nearby rivers broke their banks and parts of the city were engulfed in water. The Cumbrian capital was effectively cut off by the height of the floods, lives were lost and action has had to be taken by the council to minimise the possibility of flooding occurring again. This means that the Way will most likely be re-routed as flood defences are built.

Carlisle has always had something of a volatile history. Early occupiers included the Romans; not only did they construct Hadrian's Wall but they also built defences around the city to protect it from the onslaught of the barbarian Picts. When the Romans left the city, it was attacked and burnt by marauding Scots, to be later destroyed by the Danes. Throughout the history of Carlisle it has sustained numerous attacks and occupation by the Scots and even saw Mary, Queen of Scotland, confined in the city tower shortly before she left the region for her untimely death.

Thankfully, life is now a little quieter in the great city of Carlisle and when you do finally reach the official end of the trail at the Tourist Information Centre, you can begin to reflect on the diverse landscape, history and sensations that you have encountered and experienced along what can be considered one of the country's greatest, yet still unofficial, long distance routes - The Cumbria Way.

The autumn colours of Parsons Park Wood.

A brief clearing offers good views of the surrounding landscape before the track re-enters woodland.

The Cald Beck running through Dentonside Wood in autumn.

St Mary's Church near Sebergham.

Bell Bridge, stretching over the River Caldrew.

Ivy growing on a tree stretching over the fast rapids of the River Caldew.

The River Caldew running below Rose Bridge.

Farmers seasonal crop growing in a field near Bog Bridge.

Wild flowers near Dalston, complemented by the blue and green colours of summer.

A heavy frost transforms the landscape encountered on the Cumbria Way near the city of Carlisle.

The rising sun highlights the grandeur of Carlisle Cathedral.

Early morning winter sun illuminates the red sandstone of Carlisle Castle.

Photographer's Notes

Seventy miles is an unquestionably long distance to cover photographically. My aim with the images captured for this book was to cover every nook and cranny of the Cumbria Way's route, and hopefully to do photographic justice to the splendours to be found in the National Park and surrounding stretch of Cumbria not designated as a protected area. It was decided that every season of the year should be covered, producing a true representation of the walk for the reader at any time of the year.

Logistically this produced numerous difficulties. The only way to capture many of the images was by reaching locations on foot. This dictated carrying all my normal hiking and camping equipment, as well as heavy photographic gear including my trusty tripod – a piece of equipment that I feel is just as important as the camera itself. Over 99 per cent of the images captured for this project utilised the tripod. The cameras used were an assortment of digital and traditional film types.

The decision to make the step of using digital equipment was not one that I took lightly. There were obvious benefits such as the eradication of film and processing costs, but there were also concerns with regard to battery life, image storage and the final reproduction quality of the images. By shooting RAW files on my Cannon digital SLR, I was able to produce an image that many photographers, including myself, feel easily matches the quality produced by a traditional 35 mm camera. However, digital is somewhat of a double-edged sword, and I quickly found that I had to spend an immense amount of time editing and processing the files. Not surprising if you consider that over 1700 digital images were taken for this book.

Once I had invested in digital equipment, I decided to abandon the traditional 35 mm format and to concentrate my film captures on medium format equipment. Again, the weight of my rucksack meant that I could not physically carry a medium format SLR alongside my digital gear, so I opted to use two rangefinder cameras. The panoramic images were captured on a Hasselblad X-Pan, a unique camera hardly bigger than a 35 mm SLR yet capable of producing true panoramic images. Towards the end of the project, I upgraded my film equipment to a Mamiya 7II, a truly remarkably lightweight 6x7cm medium format rangefinder camera which offers a level of image quality that can only be exceeded by the type of large format equipment used by some of the world's greatest landscape photographers such as Ansel Adams.

Ultimately the choice of equipment is irrelevant unless you have the light – the pot of gold that every landscape photographer is constantly seeking. I have taken photographs at numerous locations around the world and I can confidently say that the quality of light to be found in the Lake District is equally as exciting as any to be found elsewhere.

Ironically, the summer months failed to provide ideal conditions, with haze in the hills reducing opportunities for vista shots. However I had the luxury of 15 months to take photographs for the book, so I could return with camera in hand to capture images when the lighting was more beneficial. Some of the shots were planned compositions, whilst others took advantage of lucky opportunities.

Using both film and digital equipment provided the means to make the most of the light and the final outcome was the coherent collection of images that you hold in your hands today. All I can say is that I hope you enjoy viewing the images as much as I enjoyed capturing them and that you will feel inspired to walk the Cumbria Way.

Canon Eos 10D,
20-35mm Lens,
Polarising Filter,
Manfrotto Tripod,
1/30 second @ f19.

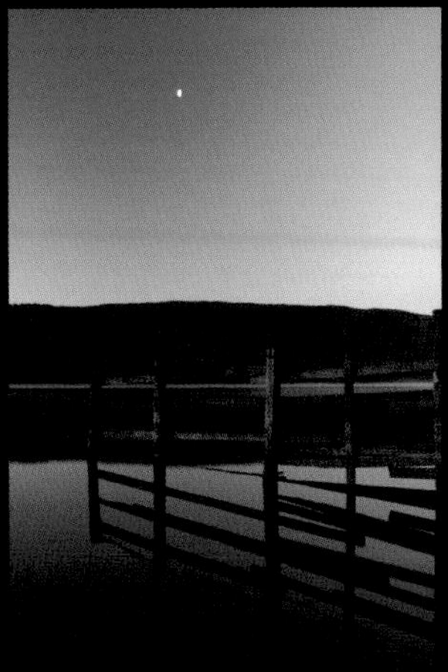

Canon Eos 20D,
20-35mm Lens,
Polarising Filter,
Manfrotto Tripod,
8 seconds @ f20.

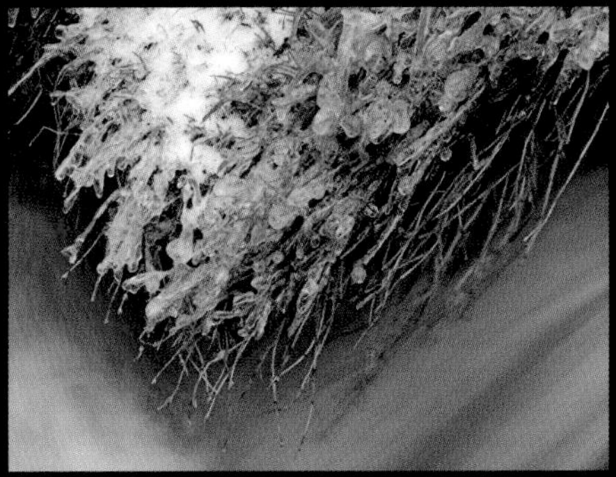

Canon Eos 20D,
75-300mm Lens,
Polarising Filter,
Manfrotto Tripod,
1 second @ f20.

Canon Eos 20D,
20-35mm Lens,
Polarising Filter,
Manfrotto Tripod,
1/15 second @ f20.

Canon Eos 20D,
20-35mm Lens,
Polarising Filter,
Manfrotto Tripod,
1/5 second @ f20.

Canon Eos 20D, 20-35mm Lens, Polarising Filter, Manfrotto Tripod, 1/6 second @ f20.

Canon Eos 10D, 20-35mm Lens, Polarising Filter, Manfrotto Tripod,
1/10 second @ f5.6

Canon Eos 20D, 20-35mm Lens,
Polarising Filter, Manfrotto Tripod,
1/6 second @ f20.

Canon Eos 10D, 20-35mm Lens, Polarising Filter, Manfrotto Tripod,
1/8 second @ f9.5

Canon Eos 20D, 20-35mm Lens, Polarising Filter, Manfrotto Tripod,
1/8 second @ f20.

Canon Eos 20D, 20-35mm Lens, Polarising Filter, Manfrotto Tripod,
1/15 second @ f20.

Canon Eos 20D, 20-35mm Lens, Polarising Filter, Manfrotto Tripod,
20 seconds @ f5.6.

Canon Eos 20D,
20-35mm Lens,
Polarising Filter,
Manfrotto Tripod,
1/13 second @ f20.

Canon Eos 20D,
20-35mm Lens,
Polarising Filter,
Manfrotto Tripod,
1/13 second @ f20.

Canon Eos 20D,
20-35mm Lens,
Polarising Filter,
Manfrotto Tripod,
1/6 second @ f22.

Hasselblad Xpan,
45mm Lens,
ND Center Spot Filter,
81B Warm up Filter,
Manfrotto Tripod,
Fujichrome Velvia.

Canon Eos 20D,
20-35mm Lens,
Polarising Filter,
Manfrotto Tripod,
1/2 second @ f20.

Canon Eos 10D,
20-35mm Lens,
Polarising Filter,
Manfrotto Tripod,
6 seconds @ f19.

Canon Eos 20D,
20-35mm Lens,
Polarising Filter,
Manfrotto Tripod,
1/2 second @ f20.

Canon Eos 20D,
20-35mm Lens,
Polarising Filter,
Manfrotto Tripod,
1/8 second @ f20.

Canon Eos 20D,
20-35mm Lens,
Polarising Filter,
Manfrotto Tripod,
1/6 second @ f22.

Canon Eos 20D,
20-35mm Lens,
Polarising Filter,
Manfrotto Tripod,
1/5 second @ f20.

Canon Eos 20D,
20-35mm Lens,
Polarising Filter,
Manfrotto Tripod,
1/10 second @ f22.

Hasselblad Xpan,
45mm Lens,
ND Center Spot Filter,
Manfrotto Tripod,
Fujichrome Velvia.

Canon Eos 20D,
20-35mm Lens,
Polarising Filter,
Manfrotto Tripod,
1/5 second @ f20.

Canon Eos 20D,
20-35mm Lens,
Polarising Filter,
Manfrotto Tripod,
1/6 second @ f22.

Canon Eos 20D,
20-35mm Lens,
Polarising Filter,
Manfrotto Tripod,
15 seconds @ f20.

Canon Eos 20D,
20-35mm Lens,
Polarising Filter,
Manfrotto Tripod,
1/8 second @ f20.

Canon Eos 20D,
75-300mm Lens,
Polarising Filter,
Manfrotto Tripod,
1/320 second @ f4.

Canon Eos 20D,
20-35mm Lens,
Polarising Filter,
Manfrotto Tripod,
1/6 second @ f20.

Canon Eos 20D,
20-35mm Lens,
Polarising Filter,
Manfrotto Tripod,
1/3 second @ f20.

Canon Eos 20D,
20-35mm Lens,
Polarising Filter,
Manfrotto Tripod,
2 seconds @ f20.

Mamiya 7ii,
80mm lens,
81B Warm up Filter,
Manfrotto Tripod,
Fujichrome Velvia.

Canon Eos 20D,
20-35mm Lens,
Polarising Filter,
Manfrotto Tripod,
1/13 second @ f20.

Canon Eos 20D,
20-35mm Lens,
Polarising Filter,
Manfrotto Tripod,
1/2 second @ f20.

Canon Eos 20D,
20-35mm Lens,
Polarising Filter,
Manfrotto Tripod,
1/13 second @ f20.

Canon Eos 300,
24mm Lens,
Warm Tone Polarising Filter,
Manfrotto Tripod,
Fujichrome Velvia.

Hasselblad Xpan, 45mm Lens,
ND Center Spot Filter,
Manfrotto Tripod,
Fujichrome Velvia.

Canon Eos 20D,
20-35mm Lens,
Polarising Filter,
Manfrotto Tripod,
2 seconds @ f20.

Canon Eos 20D,
20-35mm Lens,
Polarising Filter,
Manfrotto Tripod,
1/2 second @ f20.

Hasselblad Xpan,
45mm Lens,
ND Center Spot Filter,
81B Warm up Filter,
Manfrotto Tripod,
Fujichrome Velvia.

Canon Eos 20D,
20-35mm Lens,
Polarising Filter,
Manfrotto Tripod,
1/10 second @ f20.

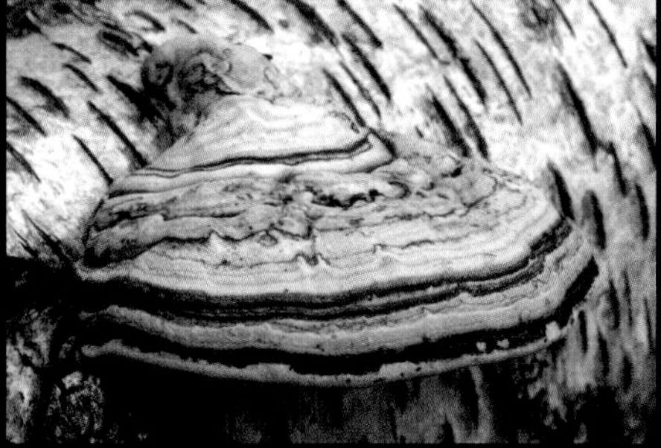

Canon Eos 20D,
75-300mm Lens,
Polarising Filter,
Manfrotto Tripod,
2 seconds @ f20.

Canon Eos 10D,
20-35mm Lens,
Polarising Filter,
Manfrotto Tripod,
10 seconds @ f13.

Canon Eos 20D,
20-35mm Lens,
Polarising Filter,
Manfrotto Tripod,
1 seconds @ f20.

Canon Eos 300,
35-80mm Lens,
Warm Tone Polarising Filter,
Manfrotto Tripod,
Fujichrome Velvia.

Canon Eos 20D,
20-35mm Lens,
Polarising Filter,
Manfrotto Tripod,
1/6 second @ f20.

Canon Eos 20D,
20-35mm Lens,
Polarising Filter,
Manfrotto Tripod,
1/2 second @ f20.

Canon Eos 20D,
20-35mm Lens,
Polarising Filter,
Manfrotto Tripod,
1/20 second @ f20.

Canon Eos 33,
20-35mm Lens,
Warm Tone Polarising Filter,
Manfrotto Tripod,
Fujichrome Velvia.

Hasselblad Xpan,
45mm Lens,
ND Center Spot Filter,
Manfrotto Tripod,
Fujichrome Velvia.

Canon Eos 20D,
20-35mm Lens,
Polarising Filter,
Manfrotto Tripod,
1 second @ f20.

Canon Eos 20D,
20-35mm Lens,
Polarising Filter,
Manfrotto Tripod,
1/10 second @ f20.

Canon Eos 10D,
20-35mm Lens,
Polarising Filter,
Manfrotto Tripod,
1/10 second @ f19.

Canon Eos 20D,
20-35mm Lens,
Polarising Filter,
Manfrotto Tripod,
1/3 second @ f20.

Canon Eos 10D,
20-35mm Lens,
Polarising Filter,
Manfrotto Tripod,
1/8 second @ f19.

Canon Eos 20D,
20-35mm Lens,
Polarising Filter,
Manfrotto Tripod,
1/25 second @ f20.

Canon Eos 10D,
20-35mm Lens,
Polarising Filter,
Manfrotto Tripod,
1/6 second @f19.

Canon Eos 10D,
20-35mm Lens,
Polarising Filter,
Manfrotto Tripod,
1/4 second @f19.

Canon Eos 10D,
20-35mm Lens,
Polarising Filter,
Manfrotto Tripod,
1/4 second @f19.

Canon Eos 10D,
20-35mm Lens,
Polarising Filter,
Manfrotto Tripod,
1/4 second @f19.

Canon Eos 20D,
20-35mm Lens,
Polarising Filter,
Manfrotto Tripod,
1/15 second @ f20.

Canon Eos 10D,
20-35mm Lens,
Polarising Filter,
Manfrotto Tripod,
1/6 second @f19.

Canon Eos 20D,
20-35mm Lens,
Polarising Filter,
Manfrotto Tripod,
1 second @ f20.

Canon Eos 10D,
20-35mm Lens,
Polarising Filter,
Manfrotto Tripod,
1/250 second @ f8.

Canon Eos 20D,
20-35mm Lens,
Polarising Filter,
Manfrotto Tripod,
1/15 second @ f20.

Canon Eos 20D,
20-35mm Lens,
Polarising Filter,
Manfrotto Tripod,
1/20 second @ f20.

Canon Eos 20D,
20-35mm Lens,
Polarising Filter,
Manfrotto Tripod,
1/10 second @ f20.

Canon Eos 20D,
20-35mm Lens,
Polarising Filter,
Manfrotto Tripod,
1/15 second @ f20.

Canon Eos 20D,
20-35mm Lens,
Polarising Filter,
Manfrotto Tripod,
1/8 second @ f20.

Canon Eos 20D,
20-35mm Lens,
Polarising Filter,
Manfrotto Tripod,
1/4 second @ f20.

Canon Eos 20D,
20-35mm Lens,
Polarising Filter,
Manfrotto Tripod,
1/5 second @ f20.

Canon Eos 20D,
20-35mm Lens,
Polarising Filter,
Manfrotto Tripod,
3 seconds @ f20.

Canon Eos 20D,
20-35mm Lens,
Polarising Filter,
Manfrotto Tripod,
1/6 second @ f20.

Canon Eos 20D,
20-35mm Lens,
Polarising Filter,
Manfrotto Tripod,
1/4 second @ f20.

Canon Eos 20D,
20-35mm Lens,
Polarising Filter,
Manfrotto Tripod,
15 seconds @ f20.

Canon Eos 20D,
20-35mm Lens,
Polarising Filter,
Manfrotto Tripod,
1 second @ f20.

Canon Eos 20D,
20-35mm Lens,
Polarising Filter,
Manfrotto Tripod,
1/4 second @ f20.

Canon Eos 20D,
20-35mm Lens,
Polarising Filter,
Manfrotto Tripod,
1/15 second @ f20.

Canon Eos 20D,
20-35mm Lens,
Polarising Filter,
Manfrotto Tripod,
1/5 second @ f20.

Canon Eos 20D,
20-35mm Lens,
Polarising Filter,
Manfrotto Tripod,
1/5 second @ f20.

Canon Eos 20D,
20-35mm Lens,
Polarising Filter,
Manfrotto Tripod,
1/3 second @ f20.

Acknowledgements

A project of this size would have not been possible without the help, advice and encouragement of numerous people from various different walks of life.

I would especially like to thank Lynette Whitehouse for accompanying me on most of the trips, assisting in the final choice of images, proof reading of the draft text, standing around in the rain, believing in me and of course carrying the tent!

Wayne Hackeson and Mark Whitehouse for being mad enough to volunteer and actually join me on some of my Cumbria Way jaunts.

David Hall at Blue Sky Images for his beautiful virtual drum scans of my medium format images.

Nick Ridley for his outstanding final design of the book and Martin Ellis at Zymurgy for making the project a reality.

Ben Barden at the Cumbria Tourist board for his encouragement, and the team at Alamy for marketing the images.

The Camping and Caravanning Club for providing me a spot to pitch my tent, and sit out the rain in Keswick!

The Ramblers Association for creating the Cumbria Way and continuing to campaign on behalf of all walkers.

My parents, John and Carol Friend, and the Whitehouse family for their support over the years.

My good friends throughout the country who have encouraged me the last two years - you know who you are!

I would also like to thank the good people of Cumbria for their famous Cumbrian hospitality and their interest and encouragement with the project. In particular I would like to thank the old lady who searched for my lost glove in a field near Caldbeck and then posted it to my home address - you really are a star!